Ava the Avocado

A Healthy Learning Paths Book

This book is dedicated to Viola and Ralph, true pioneers in healthy learning paths for children.

Sincere thanks to Dr. Jessica Wood for her artistic talent and creativity.
Special thanks to Marion and Joe who inspire others to do their best for children.

ISBN 978-0-9990550-0-7 First Edition Print, June 2017

Published by Healthy Learning Paths

When you buy this book, you support the 501(c)(3) nonprofit, Healthy Learning Paths.
Our mission is to spread the power of health for children.
Join our movement at www.healthylearningpaths.org.

Have you ever heard

Of Ava from Colorado?

She had a strange dream

That she was an avocado.

She had bright yellow eyes
And tough, dark green skin.
Her short springy legs
Trapped her hair, long and thin.

Something was not right.
Ava felt lonely and sad.
She needed some help,
So she looked for her dad.

What's on your mind?
Dad asked her politely.
Come let's take a walk,
And I'll hold your hand tightly.

Dad, I just do not know
Where to begin.
I don't understand
How I can fit in.

What happened next
Was more than just strange.
Now all shades of green,
Everything did change!

Ava looked around
And let out a scream!
It's almost as if
We are on the same team!

They walked down a path

And came to a wall

With a huge sign that read,

"Ovoids: small and TALL."

OVOIDS

Ava opened the gate

And stepped up with pride.

Can you guess what she saw?

Were ovoids inside?

(An ovoid is an object that has an egg shape.)

They strolled by the eggplants,
Tomatoes, eggs, and pears.
Ava counted the colors
And tried to hide stares.

Ava's dad took her hand,

Be careful not to fall.

You have special powers.

Let's go past this wall.

They entered a land
Where nuts, olives, and seeds
Were dancing with salmon,
While doing good deeds.

Now listen carefully
For you share these powers.
Each of these foods
Makes you healthy for hours.

Ava the Avocado,

The seeds, nuts, and fish,

All have healthy fats

For a magical dish!

Healthy fats are important.
They help children grow.
Healthy fats make you smart
And keep your skin aglow.

One thing to remember
With healthy fats you're faster,
Healthy and happy
To be your own master.

Each morning for breakfast,
The food Ava likes most
Is a big slice of avocado
On a piece of whole wheat toast!

Now you know the story
Of Ava from Colorado,
Who had a strange dream
That she was an avocado.

Ava's Guacamole

Ava says, "Nutritious and delicious! YUM!"

Food

- 2 ripe avocados
- 1 small clove of garlic
- 6 cherry or grape tomatoes
- ½ lemon

Supplies

- 1 medium bowl
- 1 spoon
- 1 knife and cutting board
- 1 lemon squeezer
- 1 mixing spoon

Step 1: Wash hands with soap and water.

Step 2: Wash avocados, garlic, tomatoes, and lemon.

Step 3: With the help of an adult, slice avocados in half.

Step 4: Use a spoon to scoop the avocado into a bowl.

Step 5: Chop the tomatoes and add to bowl.

Step 6: Use a garlic press to smash the garlic and add to bowl.

Step 7: Squeeze lemon and add 1 teaspoon of juice to bowl.

Step 8: Mash and mix well with mixing spoon.

Serve with fresh chopped vegetables like carrots, celery, bell peppers, and broccoli as a dip. This also tastes great in chicken salad, sandwiches, and wraps in place of mayonnaise.

Ava's Message

Did you know?

1. Healthy fats are needed for brain development and healthy hearts in children.
2. Some foods with healthy fats are:
   a. Avocados, olives, olive oil
   b. Fish like salmon and halibut
   c. Nuts like almonds and walnuts
   d. Sunflower and pumpkin seeds
3. What foods have unhealthy fats?
   Processed and fried foods like fast food, French fries, donuts, chips, cookies, and candy are some examples.
4. How can I recognize unhealthy fats?
   Look for trans fats, hydrogenated fats or partially hydrogenated fats on food labels.
5. When cooking meats and vegetables, think bake, broil or grill, as this is healthier than frying.

It's fun to be healthy!

Healthy, it's the new happy,

Ava the Avocado

Healthy Learning Paths was founded with a rebellious spirit and bold mission: to spread the power of health for children while leading the way for health conscious communities. We are a 501(c)(3) nonprofit organization founded by Dr. Chris Marchioni, a family medicine physician who left traditional practice to stop disease in children before it starts with our Healthy Learning Kids programs.

"While we will always need to treat disease, it is really cool to prevent disease. And, yes, we can prevent many diseases. There is no better place to start than with children," explains Dr. Marchioni.

You can help put children on the path to mental fitness, physical fitness, and social emotional fitness. Join the movement and donate at www.healthylearningpaths.org.

Made in the USA
Lexington, KY
13 December 2017